For more information on Poem Power® or
Life Transformation Resources,
please visit our web-site at:

www.lifetran.com

Poem Power®!

"A Miracle For You"

By James D. Hallinan

POEM POWER®!

Poem Power®! *The New Millennium Inspirational Poetry Series* is a Registered Trademark of James D. Hallinan.

"A Miracle For You"

By James D. Hallinan

Copyright © 2003 by James D. Hallinan

All rights reserved. No part of this book shall be reproduced or transmitted in any form or by any means, electronic, mechanical, magnetic, photographic including photocopying, recording or by any information storage and retrieval system, without prior written permission of the publisher. No patent liability is assumed with respect to the use of the information contained herein. Although every precaution has been taken in the preparation of this book, the publisher and author assume no responsibility for errors or omissions. Neither is any liability assumed for damages resulting from the use of the information contained herein.

ISBN 0-7414-1517-8

Published by:

519 West Lancaster Avenue
Haverford, PA 19041-1413
Info@buybooksontheweb.com
www.buybooksontheweb.com
Toll-free (877) BUY BOOK
Local Phone (610) 520-2500
Fax (610) 519-0261

Printed in the United States of America

Printed on Recycled Paper

Published July 2003

All photographs included in this book were taken by Jeanne M. Hallinan.

Judy and Jimmy Hallinan
Late Spring 2002 The Woodlands, Texas

Poem Power®! "A Miracle for You" - Dedication

This first volume of Poem Power® is dedicated to my sister-in-law, Judy Hallinan, who has been a blessing and inspiration to all who have known her! The first major poem I ever wrote entitled "A Miracle for You" was specifically inspired by, and written for Judy, as she embarked on the most courageous and heroic phase of her life journey, her battle against breast cancer.

To Judy, with our eternal love!

Jim, Jeanne and Jimmy Hallinan

Poem Power® Introduction

Poem Power®! "A Miracle for You" is the first volume of a planned series of poetry works to be published by inspirational writer, life/career transformation coach, and business consultant, James D. Hallinan. Poem Power® is a collection of inspirational poetry that people from all walks of life will cherish! Poem Power® captures the beauty and charm of the poetic craft with a simple yet heartfelt style and flair that will truly touch your world!

Poem Power® represents a thematically organized series of inspirational poetry utilizing fundamental life/time based periods for ongoing appreciation and reference. In this first volume of Poem Power® you will find an inspirational poem for each of the following:

Millennium
Century
Decade
Year
Each of the Four Seasons of the Year
Each of the Twelve Months of the Year

Future volumes of Poem Power® are expected to include inspirational poems for each week of the year and ultimately each and every day of the year.

Poem Power®! *"A Miracle for You"*

Inspirational Poems for the:

Millennium	A Miracle For You
Century	Timeless
Decade	Whispers From Heaven
Year	The Tree of Life

Seasons:

Spring	Silence!
Summer	Death of a Cynic
Autumn	Healing The Past
Winter	The Giving Way

Months:

January	One Second, One Seed, One Lifetime
February	My Forever Valentine
March	Oh Fiji!
April	The Sun on Cloudy Days
May	Windswept
June	Galaxies of Hidden Dreams
July	"Be"
August	Watching Dolphins Play
September	As Mysteries Unfold
October	The Stars at Night
November	Above the Clouds
December	Angel By My Side

MILLENNIUM

A Miracle for You

I hear your call from within
As difficulties near
May strength be found among jagged rocks
That trample bedlam fear
The spirit guides us with no scent
Of yonder forward ho
May faith invade your daily life
Force dwell upon ye foe
A crimson tide of grace expounds
Above the sky's outreach
Just heaven's overflow of love
Bringing peace to souls who seek

Remember life's most precious dreams
Each day above the rim
Reach up for stars of glorious feats
And always shall you win
Now time to trust the Lord above
Like you never have before
The forces gained from fortitude
Will render rightly cure
Say prayers of thanks, love, hope and peace
And know most certainly
It always seems the darkest
Just before the light that leads

Upon the wall of discontent
Lay doubting quotes of doom
But take a look around the bend
Springtime flowers bloom
May healing winds of God above
Brush gently across your brow
And cleansing waters of His grace
Be with you here and now
As near and far as the eye can see
Miracles abound
Keep the faith all your days
And one for you be found

CENTURY

Timeless

An ocean's breath of mist and waves
Scenic tides sail home
The clock struck twelve I know not when
For timeless is the moon

Timeless as when laughter falls
Cascades of love reborn
Timeless are the dreams of all
Parading through the storms

Timeless scenes of waterfalls
With no escape from mind
The universe unfolds for some
Whose timeless hearts catch fire

Timeless
Priceless is our time
No barter could be waged
Sufficient to recoup our time
Before earthly days shall fade

Timeless is my love for you
No storybook could tell
Let timeless memories prevail
Savor only deeds heartfelt

Our lives are spent possessed by time
The old and young at heart
The worries of our youth grow old
While timeless scenes depart

If only we'd make time our friend
Not foe of which to fear
Then timeless would our dreams turn true
God's presence always near

DECADE

Whispers from Heaven

Take time today to meditate and surely you shall find
Soft echoes full surrounding you as darkness turns to light
When random opportunities knock faintly at your door
Don't mistake for cynic fate, to answer is the cure

Whispers from heaven…

While accidental tourists explore lost hidden caves
A thunder bolt makes time stand still as lightning paves the way
On the brightest of the summer days, no clouds dare to appear
Yet suddenly sun showers rage and soon after rainbow cheer

Whispers from heaven…

Sometimes there seems no earthly clue
For good fortune on your doorstep
But listen closer, the message is clear
The gifts are heaven sent

Whispers from heaven
Disguised as sounds
Indecipherable to most
Only with enlightened minds
May mortals touch the Host

So remember to connect your soul
With each and all your senses
And you'll never fail to recognize
When whispers fall from heaven

YEAR

The Tree of Life

Relentless occupation with material pursuits
Blurs the boundaries between divine and ego fruits

Temptations full surround us each and every day
Time to take control, internal guidance show the way

We seem to listen lesser now
Culture drives our ears
We seek first to be understood
Without a heart for tears

Tears of others, fear and pain
We listen passively
Interjecting our own views
Before unfinished pleas

If I could rewrite history I'd start with chapter one
Eve would then repluck the fruit
From the tree, oh rightful one

Then we all would stand so pure and naked to the bone
Yet none of us could ever tell
The shame first two had known

So please take time and slow your haste
Before all time stands still
And offer helpful hands to those
Whose guilt negates free will

To just this once touch inner peace
And spread it far and wide
Like river falls that nature leaves
A world of tears subsides

The right tree is for all to choose
Of which to pick our fruit
No blame to place on those before us
The tree of life I choose

SEASONS

SPRING

Silence!

Silence!
No speak
Unease sets in
Who spills first
'Tis not a game
Solitude is king

Words
What evil
Under guise of sin
Make mention
Of retreat
The lantern guides the wind

Commotion
A traffic war
Noise pollutes the air
Dost thou protest
Nature's request
Of solemn nights despair

So peace
Surrender to yourself
That need
The first to speak

SUMMER

Death of a Cynic

What has happened to this world
The cynic's eye persuades
TV shows and radio
A fact of life these days

No tender thought to deeds well done
Let slip beyond the realm
The inner sanctum it belies
Leaves truths beyond the sun

So say you all forever days
What's lost and never won
The time to stand on scorched earth feet
Quell ye avalanche begun

But I for one tell all to hear
Of life's "just" accolades
For friends in life's true journey quest
The end of cynic ways

What legacy for gens to come
Who watch our final play
Let's pass the torch oh optimum
And death to cynic days

AUTUMN

Healing the Past

Soul searching
Soul survivors
That's what we do and are
Journey back through childhoods past
Hidden memories from afar

Take step one to heal your past
And watch the next steps flow
We must first revisit close-held pain
To reach the next plateau

So heal your past before too late
And feel the slow release
Of harbored feelings once restricting you
Now offering inner peace

Healing the past, a key to life
Discover buried scenes
Heal the past before too late
And recoup lost childhood dreams

WINTER

The Giving Way

Temper wisdom through humility
Share your knowledge freely
Contribute more than one could ask
All favors granted no strings attached

Live your life by serving others
You'll never lose yourself
God's grace avails for all to feed from
Lead others to this eternal well

A life worth living is worth remembering
Let yours be one for all ages
To impact others you've never met
A gift for true life sages

A master rules his own domain
By leaving ego far behind
Compassion leads us to our true self
Forgiving others makes souls divine

So learn to live the giving way
Let render no recourse
Find hearts fulfilled with peace and sharing
The giving way, our life support

MONTHS

JANUARY

One Second, One Seed, One Lifetime

Total consciousness
For just one second
Total clarity
Reality confronts me and I welcome it
With eyes virgin clear
Yesterday's all day haze is lifted
Like a late morn receding fog
Off a gold coast bay
Resplendent sunrays reflect my mind
The lone second builds momentum
Seconds to minutes
And minutes to hours
Hours befriend the coming days
Days to weeks, then months to years
Building bridges for a lifetime
Of purpose
One idea, the seed for future memories
The power to turn the tide
At any point and depth
Caress your seeds
Drench them with blood flowing love from your heart
For when your second arrives
Awakening you from your dark sleepless nights
You'll spot it like a shooting star
Whose hypnotic tail will pull you with it
The rush ensuing may first bewilder
But soon will soothe
Then burn to passion
Fueling your life train

One second
One seed
One lifetime

One second to awakening
One seed to enlightenment
One lifetime of passion, not born of ego
Only Love

FEBRUARY

My Forever Valentine

Majestic tides of boundless seas may never call to port
The rustic fires within my heart that yearn for your support
In times of trouble and despair I gently lay my claim
To thee dear heart, my sunset court, forever and today

There longs a passion so sincere within my aching heart
'Tis to proclaim my love for thee and never let us part
Please take my hand on cloudless days and never let it go
And join with me, our destiny, forever on life's road

Of love and life and valentines
My heart will never find
The love I've found right here with you
Of body, soul and mind
So thank you Lord for blessing me
With grace beyond so kind
But thank you most of all for
My Forever Valentine

MARCH

Oh Fiji! (Our Navini Dedication)

Bula! Bula! Bula!
Hello, welcome
We love you
Have fun
A traditional Fijian greeting
As timeless as the sun

No truer earthly paradise
Could ere be nary found
Than in the gently rolling isles
Amidst God's royal crown
Of crystal seas and virgin beaches
And cliff etched mountain sides
A virtual hypnotic trance
Blends darkness into light

Oh Fiji, God is calling you
To show the world your way
To live in all His natural wonder
Untouched by human greed decay
The lofty sun of Fiji's skies
Burns brightest in the early morn
Setting tables for a splendid day
And the clearest vision for life reborn

In Fiji you will always find
Bright smiles to match the sun
Laughter, song and kava flow
In Fiji, all day long
Fiji's people you'll quickly learn
Far outshine their sun above
Their spirit bears warm, tender hearts
Their greatest gift is love

Oh Fiji, God is calling you
To show the world His way
For Fiji, like His first pure garden
Breathes hope for all the world each day

So, vinaka vaka levu, Navini
Moce, until we meet again
You've made our honeymoon so special
Our memories of you will never end!

APRIL

The Sun on Cloudy Days

The sun surrounds us every day
An effervescent God sent light of way
No force of nature could supersede
The warmth and power that our sun breathes
But here and there the sunlight fades
On overnights and rainy days
No need to fret
The sun reappears
In fact it never disappeared

Faith in God allows one to see
The sun, when clouds may cover thee
For those who can, let see and feel
Its brilliant touch so awe-surreal
At your doorstep and morning rise
And even by your bed at night
The sun our friend always endures
At night or day, on cloudy shores

See the Son high in the sky
And during night time in your mind
Feel His ever-warm embrace
Most of all on cloudy days

MAY

Windswept

I lie awake at night humbled by the stars
The vastness of the universe lays at my beck and call
The winds build with a fury, adrift the sands ashore
My limitless boundaries fuel justly the allure
The world at night is sight unseen
Until the dawn doth wake
But lonely hearts will oft prevail
Across the windswept breaks
Time's on our side yet waits for no one
A once great prophet said
He did not sensor windswept dreams for if he did he bled
So bunker down the fortress and tighten all the chains
If destiny befalls my wishes may only love remain
Now rising star you shine so bright while glistening in the wind
Nay tell your fears to anyone, lest your dreams rescind
Master of this universe please tell us one and all
What windswept mysteries have you in store
And what may they recall
The days of future-present scenes glide idly in the night
Along the windswept house of dreams
Whose path's now wed to light
At last the calm befits my life, a stormy past behind
The windswept treasures from within can now be claimed as mine

JUNE

Galaxies of Hidden Dreams

In far off galaxies of the mind
With dark void holes so black and deep
I shiver as I seek to touch
The charred recesses so long asleep
We barely scratch our temporal surface
While revving up our "caught up" tree
How pitiful this sorry state is
To ne'er explore life's hidden dreams

Of galaxies and hidden dreams
And star crossed tales and silver screens
I've lived and learned enough to speak
Of renaissance and classic scenes

No galaxy is too far gone
From any telescopic view
It's just the same for all your dreams
First picture them in front of you
And when you first "force see" your dreams
A magnetic charm will soon appear
To pull you toward those galaxies
That once you used to fear

JULY

"BE"

No more striving
Simply "Be"

Be kindness
Be love
Be compassion
Be inspiration
Be integrity
Be gentle
Be gracious
Be humble
Be creative
Be peace
Be a leader
Be yourself
Be laughter
Be joy
Be gratitude
Be wisdom
Be authentic
Be your dreams
Be a team player
Be fun
Be imagination
Be contribution
Be respect
Be enlightened
Be sharing
Be positive
Be faith

All of these you can "Be"
And oh so many more
The choice is yours and will always "Be"
Simply "Be"
Forevermore

(To "Be" Continued!)

AUGUST

Watching Dolphins Play

Watch the dolphins frolic
And roam upon the seas so blue
No worldly care do they possess
Their spiral vaults enrapture you

The playground oceans on which they fool
Co-owned with God above
Are never purer than when they play
A study in true nature love

A dolphin's innocent portrayal
Of life's true guiding light
Brings peace to those with luck enough
To view this priceless gem so bright

A dolphin's beauty lies well beneath
Their outer rhythmic public charm
They only seek to please their master
And never hurt or ever harm

They play and pose always for free
For visitors to their vast domain
A dolphin's newborn wisdom magic
Offers respite for all those in pain

So watch the dolphins when they play
And learn from lessons their beauty sheds
To mimic dolphins, a worthy intention
Make happiness your life intent

SEPTEMBER

As Mysteries Unfold

Each day in life is precious for the mysteries it unveils
If only you will cherish it and watch as it regales
No other species near or far could ever claim this gift
Just to be called
To life's altar
And onto nature's lift

The answers to requests may come, at times unknown to all
But never let this fortune twist refuse to let you call
The rivers, trees and sunspent banks
Reply with calm salute
To questions of another time
An era once anew

The stars above, the seas below, the mountains in between
What force of nature
Only one
Could paint this awesome scene
Awash with boredom, I do say dare, how could this ere be so
With all to gaze and ponder on, life's mysteries unfold

Why waste youth on the young they say
When instinct rules the way
With just a little awe and thought, what wonders for the day
For all to see and hear and smell and taste and touch
What glee
The master ruler of your mind lays all to claim for thee

So reach beyond the sunset blue and over rainbow's gold
A treasure chest awaits for all
As life's mysteries unfold

OCTOBER

The Stars at Night

The stars at night are calling me
Their brilliance radiates the night
As evening skies fade ever slowly
The stars vanish from sight

Each star above
Reflects God's love
Beyond a daytime view
Search earnestly
Surprise your mind
The stars return
Each eve anew

Pick a star and claim your prize
Advanced of rapid falls
That wait for lonely drifting souls
Whose unseen stars miss midnight's call
When stars are ever present
Your life will soon take center stage
As stars, just like their brother sun
Transcend eternal laws of age

So remember to take time to turn
A northern scope on late day's arms
The stars bequeath their silent gifts
For those with vision charm
In the midst of God's bright glorious home
The stars share complimentary goals
Illuminating our darkest hours
The stars reflect our one true soul

The stars at night are beckoning
They wait for each of us to find
The trails they've paved with sparkling truth
The stars our friends forever shine

NOVEMBER

Above the Clouds

Flying high above the clouds
On modern era's arms
The world below
So far away
Seek refuge among the stars

No time like now to contemplate
What future's path will hold
The past and present lost in time
The frost melts days of old

A resurrection of the mind
No room for daunting doubts
That creep within our souls maligned
While hidden pearls abound

The clouds I ride on during flight
Weigh less than from below
If caught in storms far asunder
Reach above the clouds for gold

Never let one fleeting moment
Pass before your eyes
Without at least one extra step
To grasp it for all times

The clouds now mesh with scenic frames
Of worldly treasures' hue
We ride so high above the clouds
If only we all knew

DECEMBER

Angel by My Side

Once upon a time there was
An angel by my side
Not recognizable to most
But to me, she did confide

This angel was most inauspicious
At least at first I found
But after we became acquainted
Her presence was unbound

Some people don't believe in angels
Once in time, nor did I
But life's twist and turns awakened me
To my angel
By my side

Now reflecting on my life
I see shadows in the sun
No surprise for me to find
My angel was the one

With this one wish, I ask you Lord
To share this gift of thine
Let those in search of hope and comfort
Find your angels by their side

About the Writer - James D. Hallinan

Poem Power® represents Jim Hallinan's first published collection of inspirational poetry. Along with his writing endeavors, Jim is currently building a life and career coaching/training practice called Life Transformation Resources. In 1998, after a successful sixteen-year corporate career in banking, Jim moved on to pursue his own independent business activities. Since that time Jim has been involved in a variety of creative and entrepreneurial pursuits including inspirational writing; business consulting; independent sales/marketing; professional/technical writing; training and development; and information product development.

Jim lives in Glen Mills, PA with his wife Jeanne and their son Jimmy.

In the coming years look for the following Poem Power® books and related inspirational products:

Poem Power®! Volume II *Poem Power Weekly*
Poem Power®! Volume III *Poem Power Everyday*

Poem Power® Inspirational Calendars
Poem Power® Inspirational Greeting Cards
Poem Power® Inspirational Journals
Poem Power® Inspirational Bookmarks
Poem Power® Inspirational Gift Plaques

For more information on Poem Power® or
Life Transformation Resources,
please visit our web-site at:

www.lifetran.com